THE LITTLE GUIDE TO

YVES SAINT LAURENT

First published in 2024 by OH
An Imprint of HEADLINE PUBLISHING GROUP

10 9 8 7 6 5 4 3 2 1

Disclaimer:

Cataloguing in Publication Data is available from the British Library

ISBN 978-1-80069-628-0

Compiled and written by: Katie Meegan
Editorial: Saneaah Muhammad
Designed and typeset in Avenir by: Stephen Cary
Project manager: Russell Porter
Production: Arlene Lestrade
Printed and bound in China by Leo Paper Products

HEADLINE PUBLISHING GROUP
An Hachette UK Company
Carmelite House, 50 Victoria Embankment, London EC4Y 0DZ

www.headline.co.uk   www.hachette.co.uk

THE LITTLE GUIDE TO

YVES SAINT LAURENT

STYLE TO LIVE BY

Unofficial and Unauthorized

CONTENTS

INTRODUCTION

The modern wardrobe would not exist without Yves Saint Laurent. Born in Algeria to a French colonialist family, Yves Saint Laurent is, along with Coco Chanel, the most influential designer of the twentieth century. Instantly recognizable behind his thick, black-framed glasses, Saint Laurent grew from a frail fashion prodigy to towering alongside the giants of haute couture.

Saint Laurent cuts a complex figure: on the one hand, a sensitive and introverted *artiste*; on the other, a boisterous and determined *enfant terrible* who stripped off to be photographed nude to promote his own perfumes and partied with the jet-set crowd. At just twenty-one years old, he was handed the reins of the house of Dior. Before his sudden death, Christian Dior made clear his wishes for the young man to step into his shoes, calling Saint Laurent a "genius". Despite several successful collections – including the introduction of the "Trapeze" dress – Saint Laurent's appropriation of youth culture was too much for the demure clientele of Dior.

The house of Yves Saint Laurent opened in 1962, heralding an innovative new era of fashion, freed from the constraints of the past.

A revolutionary, Yves Saint Laurent is responsible for many of today's staple pieces, including the trench coat. Following in the footsteps of Coco Chanel, he adapted men's clothing for the liberated woman and created "Le Smoking", the mother of all well-cut trouser suits. He gave women confidence through the blazer by refitting the men's tuxedo jacket and sought inspiration from the military, creating the safari jacket and the jumpsuit. Saint Laurent blended the worlds of art and fashion, seeking inspiration in the geometric shapes of the cubist paintings of Piet Mondrian, the vibrant colours of the pop art movement and the opulence of Tsarist Russia and the ballet.

Yves Saint Laurent shaped the attitude of women in the latter half of the twentieth century – an attitude of freedom, elegance and confidence in oneself.

CHAPTER ONE

BEGINNINGS OF YVES

FROM HIS EARLY CHILDHOOD
IN ALGERIA, IT WAS CLEAR
THAT YVES SAINT LAURENT
WAS DESTINED FOR
GREATNESS, RISING QUICKLY
THROUGH THE RANKS OF
THE PRESTIGIOUS COUTURE
HOUSE OF CHRISTIAN DIOR.

I felt myself drawn to the past, whilst the future drove me ahead.

Yves Saint Laurent on what inspired his career, as quoted in Emma Baxter-Wright, *Little Book of Yves Saint Laurent*, 2021.

My mother spent nearly all her time dressing up. I was fascinated by the dresses she wore every evening.

Yves crediting his mother for instilling a sense of style in him from an early age, as quoted in the documentary *Yves Saint Laurent, Tout Terriblement* by Jérôme de Missolz, 1994.

I can still see my mother, about to leave for a ball, come to kiss me goodnight, wearing a long dress of white tulle with pear-shaped white sequins.

As seen on dazeddigital.com by Susannah Frankel, March 21, 2014.

When he was three, he changed the way my aunt dressed… he didn't like the dress she was wearing. She changed it! At three years old, he already had that instinct.

Lucienne

Saint Laurent's mother recalling his early interest in fashion, as quoted in the documentary *Yves Saint Laurent, 5 avenue Marceau, 75116 Paris* by David Teboul, 2002.

Yves Henri Donat Mathieu-Saint-Laurent was born in the city Oran, Algeria.

The eldest of three children, Yves was raised in a loving household by his mother, the glamourous and cultured Lucienne, and father, Charles, an industrialist.

My father… was an exceptional human being. I was like God Almighty for him. There was extraordinary kindness.

Yves Saint Laurent also had a close relationship with his father, who never doubted his creative genius, as quoted in the documentary *Yves Saint Laurent, Tout Terriblement* by Jérôme de Missolz, 1994.

My father adored me. On the last day of his life, his last words were 'Where's Yves?'

As quoted in the documentary *Yves Saint Laurent, 5 avenue Marceau, 75116 Paris* by David Teboul, 2002.

We lived in a big, three-story house in Oran and were a very jolly family.

Yves Saint Laurent recalls his loving family environment in an interview with Yvonne Baby, *Le Monde*, December 8, 1983.

When you live in the provinces, magazines from the capital are hugely important. At the time there were fantastic magazines about the theatre, and also fashion magazines with designs by people like Bérard, Dalí, Cocteau. Those magazines had an enormous influence on me.

As quoted in Emma Baxter-Wright, *Little Book of Yves Saint Laurent*, 2021.

"

Yves was always interested in
fashion… We bought all the papers:
Vogue, L'Illustration and *Le Jardin
des Modes*. He did the sets of
the Yacht Club and receptions and
costumes for the dance school.

"

Lucienne

On Saint Laurent's interest in fashion from an early age, as quoted
in an interview with Michèle Sider, *Femme*, March 1992.

"

I think of myself as a Frenchman
born in Algeria.

"

Yves Saint Laurent on his identity, as quoted in *Yves Saint Laurent,
5 avenue Marceau, 75116 Paris* by David Teboul, 2002.

The Mathieu-Saint-Laurent family split their time between their villa in Oran and a summer home in the French seaside retreat of Trouville.

Part of refined society, Yves was continuously exposed to discussions of the latest fashions, plays and cultural movements of the day.

I told myself repeatedly 'one day you will be famous'.

As seen on dazeddigital.com by Susannah Frankel,
March 21, 2014.

As a child, I was very sensitive
and very happy. I had a wonderful
childhood.

Yves Saint Laurent on his happy childhood in the
documentary *Yves Saint Laurent, 5 avenue Marceau, 75116 Paris*
by David Teboul, 2002.

I had just blown out the candles of the cake when, with a second gulp of breath, I hurled my secret wish across a table surrounded by loving relatives: 'My name will be written in fiery letters on the Champs Elysees'.

As seen on dazeddigital.com by Susannah Frankel, March 21, 2014.

At the age of twelve, Yves was sent to a Jesuit-Catholic boarding school.

A shy and artistic boy, he unfortunately often found himself the target of bullies.

These difficult childhood experiences would continue to haunt him in his adult years.

66

The true paradises are the
paradises that we have lost.

99

Marcel Proust

A quote from *Le Temps Retrouvé* (1927). Saint Laurent drew
great inspiration from Proust; he shares this quote while
reminiscing about his childhood in the documentary *Yves Saint
Laurent, 5 avenue Marceau, 75116 Paris* by David Teboul, 2002.

On the one hand, at home there was joy and the world I dreamed up in my drawings, sets, costumes and theater; at Catholic school, on the other hand, there were tests and a world I was excluded from.

Yves recalls his struggles during his teenage years in an interview with Yvonne Baby, *Le Monde*, December 8, 1983.

My classmates could see I was not similar. So they made me their scapegoat. They hit me or locked me in the toilets. During the break I would take refuge in the chapel or I would arrange to stay alone in the classroom.

Yves on the bullying he received from classmates at the boarding school he attended from twelve years old. As seen on dazeddigital.com by Susannah Frankel, March 21, 2014.

When I was 14, I imagined that
I had a couture house on Place
Vendôme… I played the 'grand
couturier'.

Bullying did not stop Yves dreaming of greatness.
As quoted in *Yves Saint Laurent, 5 avenue Marceau, 75116 Paris*
by David Teboul, 2002.

Inspired by plays that he had seen and illustrations from fashion magazines, Yves began to draw sets and costumes for imaginary theatre and ballet performances.

Now showcased in the YSL museum in Paris, these sketches date back to 1951 and were signed "Yves Mathieu Saint Laurent" or "YMSL", changing to "YSL" around 1957.

Yves a soldier? You might as well try changing a swan into a crocodile!

Victoire Doutreleau

The Dior model and muse for Saint Laurent recalls the shock of Saint Laurent's conscription to the French army. As cited in Laurence Benaïm, *Yves Saint Laurent*, 1993.

In 1953, at the age of just 17, Yves Saint Laurent placed third in the Secrétariat International de la Laine design competition.

The following year he won the same competition, prompting his move to Paris at 18 years old to begin an illustrious career.

An ugly, ungainly, overgrown boy with thick glasses, and so horribly shy he couldn't take his eyes off the floor.

A rather unflattering description of a young Saint Laurent by a journalist upon his win at the Secrétariat International de la Laine design competition at 18 years old. As seen on guardian.com by John-Michael O'Sullivan, March 2, 2014.

33

Struck by the similarities between Yves Saint Laurent's designs and those of Christian Dior, the editor-in-chief of *Vogue Paris*, Michel de Brunhoff, connected the teenager with the venerated designer.

Yves began work as an assistant in the studio of Christian Dior in the summer of 1955.

"

I have never in my life met anyone
more gifted. If the young man
grows up to become a great man,
have a thought for me...

"

Michel de Brunhoff

De Brunhoff, editor-in-chief of *Vogue* (*Paris*), introduced Saint
Laurent to Dior in 1955. As seen on museeyslparis.com.

My first dress was made by Hubert de Givenchy. I've always considered him a great couturier.

Saint Laurent discusses the winning dress that launched his career in haute couture. As quoted in *Yves Saint Laurent, 5 avenue Marceau, 75116 Paris* by David Teboul, 2002.

66

Yves Saint Laurent is young, but he is an immense talent. In my last collection, I consider him to be the father of 34 out of the 180 designs. I think the time has come to reveal it to the press. My prestige won't suffer from it.

99

Christian Dior

Revealing Saint Laurent's talent to a business partner in 1957.
Saint Laurent spent two years working alongside Christian Dior.
As seen on museeyslparis.com.

Dior fascinated me. I couldn't speak in front of him. He taught me the basis of my art. Whatever was to happen next, I never forgot the years I spent at his side.

Yves Saint Laurent on working for his idol, Christian Dior.
As quoted on brisbanetimes.com by Dominique Ageorges,
June 2, 2008.

It would not be surprising if this boy of 23 felt the burden of embodying the house of Dior.

In 1959, already two years into his tenure a creative director of Dior, a journalist notes the immense pressure that such a young designer must be under. As seen on theguardian.com, November 18, 2013.

66

He taught me the essential. Then came other influences that, because he had taught me the essential, blended into this essential and found it to be a wonderful and prolific terrain, the necessary seeds that would allow me to assert myself, grow strong, blossom and finally exude my own universe.

99

In 1986, Yves Saint Laurent reflects on the teachings he received from Dior, as seen on museeyslparis.com.

Saint Laurent is the only one
worthy to carry on after me.

Christian Dior

As cited on telegraph.com, June 1, 2008.

CHAPTER
TWO

COLOURS AND LINES

UNDER THE TUTELAGE OF DIOR, YVES SAINT LAURENT THRIVED. HOWEVER, IT WAS UPON DIOR'S DEATH AND SAINT LAURENT RESUMING THE POSITION OF CREATIVE DIRECTOR AT DIOR THAT HE BEGAN TO EXPERIMENT WITH REVOLUTIONARY COLOURS AND SHAPES.

SAINT LAURENT'S UNIQUE APPROACH TO SUCH ELEMENTS CONTINUED THROUGHOUT HIS CAREER.

Fashion fades, style is eternal.

An iconic quote by Yves Saint Laurent, as seen on harpersbazaar.com, July 9, 2015.

I do not decide that skirts shall be short or long. The shape of the dress itself often dictates the length.

99

As seen on theguardian.com, November 18, 2013.

I love black because it affirms,
designs and styles. A woman in a
black dress is a pencil stroke.

As seen on anothermag.com by Daisy Woodward,
August 1, 2017.

Yves has a phenomenal sense
of colour, but he needs me to jerk
it out of his system.

LouLou de la Falaise

Yves Saint Laurent's long-time muse and collaborator
on his relationship with colour. As cited in theguardian.com
by Lauren Cochrane, May 2, 2018.

I tried to show that fashion is an art. For that, I followed the counsel of my master Christian Dior and the imperishable lesson of Mademoiselle Chanel. I created for my era and I tried to foresee what tomorrow would be.

"

As seen on vogue.com, August 1, 2013.

Dior was an inspiration and mentor to the young Saint Laurent throughout the early part of his career.

The pair worked so closely together that Saint Laurent was named Dior's successor upon his sudden death in 1957.

At the age of just 21, Saint Laurent took over as artistic director of haute couture for Dior.

My dream is to provide women
with the foundations of a classic
wardrobe that escapes
the fashion of the moment,
giving them greater confidence
in themselves.

As quoted in Emma Baxter-Wright, *Little Book of Yves Saint Laurent*, 2021.

"

In that first suitcase, there
was everything. Rigor. Shape.
Transparency. An outline.

"

Anne-Marie Muñoz

A long-time collaborator with Saint Laurent, Anne-Marie describes
his first solo collection under Dior, as seen on museeyslparis.com.

I was stuck in a traditional form
of elegance, and Courrèges
took me out of it. His collection
energized me. I told myself,
'I can find better'.

Saint Laurent on fellow couturier André Courrèges,
whom he credits with shaking up the silhouette of the time.
As seen on museeyslparis.com.

Still grieving the loss of his mentor Dior, Yves Saint Laurent launched his first show under Dior's name on January 30, 1958, to great commercial and critical acclaim.

His debut collection, named "Trapeze", was a youthful departure from the narrow-waisted silhouettes of Dior's "New Look".

Artistically… When I started
I was very young… I started with
Christian Dior. He taught me the
business, a way of seeing fabric…
Yes, there are things one learns
from others. I don't think one can
be alone, always alone; I mean in
one's field, it's not possible.

As quoted in an interview with Bianca Jagger, *Interview
Magazine*, January 1973.

In the winter of 1960, Saint Laurent was drafted into the French army to fight in the Algerian colonial war.

He collapsed during initial training and was seconded to a psychiatric hospital.

Impacted by this ordeal, he was cared for by his partner, Pierre Bergé.

Before, I used only dark tones. Then Morocco came along with its colours… those of the earth and the sand.

Yves Saint Laurent on the influence of Moroccan culture, as seen on cabanamagazine.com by Francesca Simpson, January 2023.

On every street corner in Marrakech, you encounter astonishingly vivid groups of men and women, which stand out in a blend of pink, blue, green and purple caftans.

Yves Saint Laurent on the influence of the colours of Marrakech in his work, as seen on museeyslparis.com.

With the support and business acumen of his partner Pierre Bergé, Yves Saint Laurent realized his dream of opening his own couture house.

In December 1961, the house of Yves Saint Laurent opened for the first time on 30 bis Rue Spontini, Paris.

Playing with fashion is an art.

As quoted in Diana Vreeland et al., *Yves Saint Laurent*, 1983.

Leafing through a book that his mother had given him for Christmas, Saint Laurent stumbled upon the work of Dutch painter Piet Mondrian.

Struck by Mondrian's use of colour and lines, Saint Laurent produced 26 new designs in a matter of weeks.

The 1965 "Ligne Mondrian" was received with global acclaim.

Mondrian is purity, and you can't go any further in painting. The masterpiece of the twentieth century is a Mondrian.

Yves Saint Laurent on the significance of Mondrian's art, as seen on museeyslparis.com.

"

Not only does fashion accurately reflect an era, it is also one of the more direct forms of visual expression in human culture.

"

Piet Mondrian

The Dutch cubist painter Piet Mondrian was the guiding inspiration behind the Autumn/Winter 1965 collection. The "Mondrian" cocktail dresses, shift-like with block primary colours, became synonymous with YSL. As seen on museeyslparis.com.

Contrary to what people might think, the severe lines of Mondrian's pictures worked well on the female form. The results provoked a sensation.

Yves Saint Laurent on Mondrian as an inspiration, in an interview with *Paris Match*, 1981.

I suddenly realized that dresses should no longer be composed of lines, but colours.

Yves Saint Laurent on the "Mondrian" collection. Taken from an article by Frederique Van Reij, *The Rijks Museum Bulletin*, December 2012.

Mondrian was my last minute inspiration… It wasn't until I opened a Mondrian book my mother had given me for Christmas that I hit on the key idea.

As seen on anothermag.com by Jack Moss, February 1, 2018.

I realized that we had to stop conceiving of a garment as sculpture and that, on the contrary, we had to view it as a mobile.
I realized that fashion had been rigid up till then, and that we now have to make it move.

Taken from an article by Frederique Van Reij, *The Rijks Museum Bulletin*, December 2012.

"

This is the dress of tomorrow.

"

Harper's Bazaar

On the 1965 "Mondrian" dress, as seen on anothermag.com
by Jack Moss, February 1, 2018.

Seeing Cubism paintings at the Beaubourg makes me very happy, and also old films.

Saint Laurent on his love of Cubist painting, the movement that Mondrian was a part of, in an interview with *Dazed & Confused*, March 2000.

❝

He used colours the way a sensitive collagist might – full blown, in unusual combinations.

❞

Richard Martin

The curator of the Metropolitan Museum's Costume Institute on Saint Laurent, after staging a retrospective of his work in 1983. As quoted in *Los Angeles Times* by Geraldine Baum, September 15, 1994.

CHAPTER THREE

WEARING INNOVATION

YVES SAINT LAURENT WAS
A RULE-BREAKER. IN THE SPIRIT
OF THE "SWINGING SIXTIES",
HE EMBRACED THE FASHIONS OF
THE STREET, INTRODUCING READY-
TO-WEAR PIECES THAT WERE
ACCESSIBLE TO THOUSANDS.

HE SOUGHT INSPIRATION
FROM TRADITIONALLY MASCULINE
SHAPES, CREATING
"LE SMOKING" TROUSER SUIT,
"LE TRENCH", SAFARI JACKETS
AND JUMPSUITS.

The big difference between couture and ready-to-wear is not design. It is the fabrics, the handwork and the fittings.
The act of creation is the same.

Saint Laurent speaks to *Women's Wear Daily* in 1968 about the difference between traditional high fashion and prêt-à-porter (ready-to-wear).

I wanted women to have the
same basic wardrobe as a man.
Blazer, trousers and suit. They're
so functional. I believed women
wanted this and was right.

As quoted in an interview with *The Observer*, June 1997.

66

Fashion is a reflection of its time.

99

Yves Saint Laurent on the evolving nature of fashion,
as quoted in an article by *The New York Times*,
February 19, 1971.

In 1960, Yves Saint Laurent took inspiration from the jazz clubs and beatniks of Paris for the "Beat" collection.

This youthful style was too much of a sharp departure for Dior's more distinguished clientele, soon marking the end of Yves Saint Laurent's time with the House of Dior.

"

Saint Laurent designs for women with a double life. His clothes for daywear help women to enter a world full of strangers. They enable her to go wherever she wants without arousing unwelcome attention, thanks to their somehow masculine quality. However, for the evening, when she may choose her company, he makes her seductive.

"

Catherine Deneuve

The close friend, actress and muse of Yves Saint Laurent discusses his duality. As seen on anothermag.com by Daisy Woodward, August 1, 2017.

"

I detest fashion ultimately.
I adore clothes but I hate fashion.

"

As quoted in an interview with Bianca Jagger, *Interview Magazine*, January 1973.

Good clothing is a passport
for happiness.

As seen on anothermag.com by Daisy Woodward,
August 1, 2017.

Freed from the constraints of Dior's traditions, YSL burst onto the fashion scene.

In just a handful of seasons, Saint Laurent debuted a spate of now-classic pieces, including the double-breasted pea coat, tunic shifts, "sailor" trousers and, of course, the eponymous trench coat.

The ready-to-wear is not a poor substitute for couture. It is the future. We know that we are dressing younger, more receptive women. With them it is easy to be bolder.

As quoted in Laurence Benaïm, *Yves Saint Laurent*, 1993.

I'm constantly looking for perfection.

As quoted in an interview with Bianca Jagger, *Interview Magazine*, January 1973.

66

It's a love story between couture and me.

99

As quoted in an interview with *Dazed & Confused*, March 2000.

Haute couture consists of secrets whispered from generation to generation.

As seen on anothermag.com by Daisy Woodward, August 1, 2017.

The Autumn/Winter 1965 collection marked a turning point in Saint Laurent's creative trajectory.

Stimulated by the work of fellow Parisian couturier Courrèges, Saint Laurent scrapped the majority of his designs just weeks before they were due to be shown.

Who most impressed me? There are many… But I think, finally, one learns most from oneself, from personal experience.

As quoted in an interview with Bianca Jagger, *Interview Magazine*, January 1973.

What will be more and more
important is to be able to create,
through a style, clothing that won't
go out of style...

As quoted in an article by David Livingstone,
FASHION Magazine, 1982.

Interviewer: Do you have any regrets?
YSL: Not to have invented denim.

As quoted in an interview with *Dazed & Confused*, March 2000.

I wish I had invented blue jeans.
They have expression, modesty, sex
appeal, simplicity: all I hope for in
my clothes.

As seen on anothermag.com by Daisy Woodward,
August 1, 2017.

Saint Laurent continued his groundbreaking work with his 1966 collections.

Influenced by the pop art movement, he showcased cocktail dresses in a vibrant range of colours and graphic designs.

I think there are three kinds of
designers. The big ones, the real
ones and those who know how to
strike a chord with a woman just
by making a very simple dress or
a very simple suit.

As cited in Jean-Christophe Napias and Patrick Mauriès,
The World According to Yves Saint Laurent, 2023.

The most beautiful clothes that can dress a woman are the arms of the man she loves. But for those who haven't had the fortune of finding this happiness, I am there.

As seen on anothermag.com by Daisy Woodward, August 1, 2017.

Saint Laurent realized that the youth of the day no longer wanted to be fitted in stuffy ateliers, but were seeking more affordable, accessible routes to couture.

In September 1966, the first Rive Gauche boutique opened in Paris, selling seasonal ready-to-wear clothes, using YSL's signature designs made with quality fabrics.

I prefer my look to be in my Rive Gauche collections rather than in the couture four months later... [Fashion is] what you see in the street, what women buy and wear, what is copied. It's ready-to-wear.

As quoted in an article by David Livingstone, *FASHION Magazine*, 1982.

A woman in a pantsuit is not masculine at all. A severe and implacable cut only emphasises her femininity, her seductiveness, all the more. I had noticed men were much more confident in their clothes. So I sought through trouser suits, trench coats, tuxedos and pea coats to give women the same confidence.

As seen on thenationalnews.com by Sarah Maisey, October 7, 2017.

I chose this pantsuit in my last collection; it is a real men's suit to represent the women of the future. I think that in twenty years it will still be just right.

As seen on cabanamagazine.com by Francesca Simpson, January 2023.

Young people, they don't have
any memories.

"

Saint Laurent dismissed criticism of his 1940s-inspired
"Scandal" collection by aiming it towards a younger audience,
as quoted in an interview with *Vogue France*, March 1971.

YSL's Rive Gauche Parisian boutique was an instant success.

Soon the concept of ready-to-wear designer clothes was replicated in Rive Gauche shops in New York and London.

Saint Laurent soon turned his attention to menswear, opening the first YSL men's boutique in 1969.

I would very much like to write a book… A very, very beautiful book that would be a summation of everything I love, of all my thoughts about life, women, men, beauty… It would be a memoir… but I don't have the patience right now to write it. I'm waiting 'til I have time.

As quoted in an interview with Bianca Jagger, *Interview Magazine*, January 1973.

At moments what comes out is delirious. It's going to be quite a book. It's ambitious. Like me. It must never be finished.

Throughout his career, Saint Laurent expressed interest in writing a memoir, as quoted in an interview with *The Observer*, June 1997.

Dressing is a way of life. It brings you joy. It can give you freedom and liberation, help you to find yourself and move without restraint.

As quoted in Diana Vreeland et al., *Yves Saint Laurent*, 1983.

Throughout the 1960s and 1970s, Saint Laurent embraced his position as both creative director and celebrity figurehead of YSL.

Despite struggles with addiction and depression, he could often be found dancing until the early hours of the morning in Paris's most exclusive nightclubs.

To Saint Laurent, the city's thriving nightlife was both a source of inspiration and excess.

CHAPTER
FOUR

SCENTS AND SCANDAL

EVER THE RULE-BREAKER, YVES
SAINT LAURENT WAS NEVER ONE
TO SHY AWAY FROM SCANDAL.

WHETHER IT WAS CREATING THE
FIRST TROUSERS WIDELY WORN BY
WOMEN, INVOKING A PAST THAT
FRANCE WOULD RATHER FORGET,
OR POSING NAKED TO PROMOTE
HIS OWN PERFUME, SAINT
LAURENT CERTAINLY KNEW HOW
TO GET PEOPLE TALKING.

So they have crowned me king.
Look what happened to the other
kings of France.

As quoted in an interview at the height of Saint Laurent's
career, 1968.

"

I detest courtiers who confuse their work with art. Courtier, haute couture, mode – all these terms are *passé*.

"

As quoted in an article by David Livingstone, *FASHION Magazine*, 1982.

What do I want? To shock people, to force them to think.

As seen on forbes.com by Cecilia Rodriguez, February 10, 2015.

I don't care if my pleated or draped dresses evoke the 1940s for cultivated fashion people. What's important is that young girls who have never known this fashion want to wear them.

Saint Laurent reflects on the backlash he received for the 1971 "Scandal" collection, as quoted in an interview with *Elle Magazine*, 1971.

"

It was the collection that everyone
calls 'kitsch' (I hate that word)...
That was a reaction against the turn
fashion had taken... the gypsies,
all those long skirts and bangles...
so I did my collection as a kind of
humorous protest, only everyone
took it seriously.

"

Further backlash that Saint Laurent received for the 1971
"Scandal" collection, as seen in anothermag.com by Osman
Ahmed, November 30, 2015.

Yves Saint Laurent and Pierre Bergé made their first trip to Morocco in 1966.

Falling in love with the country, they purchased Dar el-Hanch, otherwise known as "the Snake House".

Saint Laurent would visit Marrakech several times a year, finding creative inspiration in the colourful landscape and traditional clothing of northern Africa.

I cannot pretend to do sculpture
and make a woman the ridiculous
pedestal of my pretensions.

Yves Saint Laurent drew huge inspiration from contemporary art
and had many musings over the relationship between high fashion
and fine art. Taken from an article by Frederique Van Reij,
The Rijks Museum Bulletin, December 2012.

Haute couture secretes nothing
but nostalgia and restrictions.
Like an old woman.

As seen on thecut.com by Sarah Moroz, April 8, 2015.

In his Autumn/Winter 1966 collection, Saint Laurent introduced what would one day become a classic piece: the tuxedo.

Named "Le Smoking", Saint Laurent adapted the traditionally masculine suit to fit the female form.

The tuxedo jacket would then go on to feature in every single one of YSL's collections until 2002.

The smoking jacket... gave freedom to the woman. It also gave the woman the confidence to feel beautiful.

Saint Laurent on "Le Smoking" jacket, his most cherished design, in an interview with *Dazed & Confused*, March 2000.

Isn't that the truth; people are boring when we're sure of them.

As quoted in an interview with Bianca Jagger, *Interview Magazine*, January 1973.

We must never confuse elegance
with snobbery.

An iconic quote by Yves Saint Laurent, as seen in huffpost.com
by Sarah Leon, October 3, 2012.

Elegance is a dress too dazzling to dare to wear it twice. I like eccentricity, everything that is fun, the unexpected.

As seen on cabanamagazine.com by Francesca Simpson, January 2023.

Saint Laurent has excellent taste.
The more he copies me the better
taste he displays.

Coco Chanel

As seen on wwd.com by Layla Ilchi, August 19, 2019.

As well as feminizing the tuxedo jacket, Saint Laurent also sought inspiration from masculine elements through the appropriation of the military-style "Saharienne" safari jacket.

Now considered a classic YSL piece, the first safari jacket was created for a *Vogue Paris* feature in 1967.

Nothing is more beautiful than a naked body.

As seen on showstudio.com, January 27, 2022.

Along with the safari jacket, Saint Laurent debuted the jumpsuit in the Spring/Summer 1968 collection.

Again inspired by military wear, Saint Laurent tailored the jumpsuit to hug the curves of the female form.

❝

I'm very sure of myself – what I do and what I like.

❞

As quoted in an interview with Bianca Jagger, *Interview Magazine*, January 1973.

I like luxury only when it is pared down. A girl in a black tuxedo. A long black jersey dress in the middle of a crowd of embroidery and sequins. People are always too overdressed.

As cited in Jean-Christophe Napias and Patrick Mauriès, *The World According to Yves Saint Laurent*, 2023.

Inspired by the vintage style of model/designer Paloma Picasso, Saint Laurent turned to 1940s style for the 1971 "Liberation" collection.

Met with widespread disapproval from clientele and the media, the show was quickly dubbed the "Scandal" collection.

I wanted a lush, heavy and languid perfume. I wanted Opium to be captivating, and I wanted its scent to evoke everything I like: the sophisticated Orient, imperial China and exoticism.

As quoted in an article by *Women's Wear Daily*, September 18, 1978.

"

[He] gave his pan-generational
clients an unparalleled assurance
and an insouciant panache –
sex appeal without vulgarity.

"

Hamish Bowles

As seen on vogue.com.au by Sam Rogers, July 28, 2019.

I have sought for purity, but I have interjected unexpected accessories: pointed collars, little hats, shoes with pompons. With these kinds of winks, I wanted to bring a little humour to haute couture.

Saint Laurent on the importance of accessories, as quoted in Diana Vreeland, et al., *Yves Saint Laurent*, 1983.

Creating scandals appeared to be a profitable approach for YSL. So much so that in 1971, Saint Laurent approached photographer Jeanloup Sieff with a novel idea to promote the new fragrance *Pour Homme*.

The designer was photographed nude, aside from his trademark glasses. Apart from *Vogue* and *Paris Match*, no other publication would print it, causing a stir and curiosity in the consumer.

He told me to photograph him in the nude, he said he wanted to create a scandal. It was all Yves's idea.

Jeanloup Sieff

Photographer of the scandalous *Pour Homme* fragrance campaign, where he photographed Saint Laurent in the nude for publicity, as quoted in Emma Baxter-Wright, *Little Book of Yves Saint Laurent*, 2021.

The most beautiful makeup is passion, but cosmetics are easier to buy.

As seen on vogue.pt, April 14, 2022.

"

It was just a provocation on the part of Yves Saint Laurent. The picture didn't specifically target the gay population, even though it resonated strongly among them. In any case the photo was hardly published at the time. Just barely in the French press. It was only much later on that it became an almost mythical icon.

"

Pierre Bergé

Recalling the *Pour Homme* scandal in an interview with *Dutch Magazine*, 1997.

One can never overstate the importance of accessories.

Quoted by Yves Saint Laurent in 1977, as seen on refinery29.com by Landon Peoples, May 11, 2018.

I never thought the appearance
of a true woman would provoke
such a scandal.

As quoted in an article by *The New York Times*,
February 19, 1971.

Marked by plunging necklines, square shoulders and red lipstick, the "Scandal" collection ruffled the feathers of YSL's now middle-aged haute couture clientele.

Saint Laurent was accused of glorifying a not-so-distant past and painful memories of Paris under Nazi occupation.

I love simple dresses and crazy accessories.

As seen on vogue.fr by Alexandre Marain,
September 25, 2017.

Despite being critiqued as "kitsch", the backlash against the "Scandal" collection was intense but short-lived.

Saint Laurent again proved to be a trailblazer, representing a younger generation who casually mixed eras, influences and cultures.

CHAPTER
FIVE

A WORLD OF INSPIRATION

YVES SAINT LAURENT
CONSTANTLY SOUGHT INSPIRATION
FROM THE WORLD AROUND HIM,
SEAMLESSLY BLENDING
STREETWEAR WITH HIGH ART,
RETRO SHAPES WITH OVERT
MODERNITY AND THEATRE AND
BALLET WITH EASTERN
FOLKLORE.

If I wasn't a couturier I would have probably devoted myself to the theatre. The theatre's spell has appeared as a livelier, more radiant refuge than reality.

As quoted in Emma Baxter-Wright, *Little Book of Yves Saint Laurent*, 2021.

I approached every country
through dreams.

Yves Saint Laurent on drawing inspiration from Eastern cultures,
as seen on theguardian.com by Susie Lau, October 2, 2018.

At the age of 13 in Oran, where I was born, I saw a performance of [Molière's] *École des femmes* (School for Wives) starring Louis Jouvet. The set was by Christian Bérard, an immense artist.
It had a major impact me.

Saint Laurent on his early encounters with theatre and how it inspired him. As seen on museeyslparis.com.

I don't know if this is my best collection, but it is my most beautiful collection.

Saint Laurent speaks to *The New York Times* upon the release of the 1976 "Opéra-Ballets Russes" collection, inspired by Tsarist Russia and the ballet.

Interviewer: What is your most beautiful memory in your thirty years of designing?

YSL: The collection inspired by Russia. Perhaps it wasn't the most successful one, but it was wonderfully received at a time when the world condemned opulence. And it was opulent.

As quoted in an interview with *Vogue*, September 1976.

In 1971, Bianca Pérez-Mora Macías commissioned a wedding dress for her upcoming nuptials to Rolling Stones frontman, Mick Jagger.

A trendsetter in her own right, Bianca and Yves created one of the most iconic wedding outfits of the twentieth century.

The sharp-shouldered, white tuxedo suit worn with an oversized sun hat was soon splashed across front pages all over the world.

Over the years, I have learned that what is important in a dress is the woman who is wearing it.

As seen on glamour.com by Kristi Kellogg, February 10, 2020.

Each model I have represents a type
of ideal woman to me.

As quoted in an interview with Bianca Jagger, *Interview
Magazine*, January 1973.

If you don't have the power
of imagination, you don't have
anything.

As quoted in an interview with *Women's Wear Daily*, 1978.

A good model can advance fashion by ten years.

As seen on anothermag.com by Daisy Woodward, August 1, 2017.

I have never been able to work
on a wooden mannequin;
I play by unrolling the fabric on
the model, walking around her,
making her move.

"

As quoted in *Paris Match* by Irène Vacher, December 4, 1981.

To serve women's bodies, their gestures, their attitude, their lives. I wanted to be part of the women's liberation movement of the past century.

Yves Saint Laurent on his designs being influenced by the changing roles of women. As seen on theglossarymagazine.com by Harriet Cooper, May 7, 2020.

Father of pop art Andy Warhol asked Yves Saint Laurent to sit for a series of multicoloured silk screen portraits in 1972.

Their friendship endured decades, with Warhol even creating portraits of the couturier's bulldog Moujik in 1986.

The best suits since Chanel.

Life Magazine

On the first collection of suits created by Yves Saint Laurent,
March 2, 1962.

If I had to choose a design among all those that I have presented, it would unquestionably be the tuxedo jacket… And since then, it has been in every one of my collections. It is in a sense the 'label' of Yves Saint Laurent.

Yves Saint Laurent reflects on his achievements, as quoted in *Paris Match* by Irène Vacher, December 4, 1981.

I was deeply struck by a photograph of Marlene Dietrich wearing men's clothes. A tuxedo, a blazer or a naval officer's uniform – any of them. A woman dressed as a man must be at the height of femininity to fight against a costume that isn't hers.

As quoted in an interview with *Vogue Paris*, December 1983.

People have to change their
own lives, minds and manner of
living before they can change
their clothes.

As cited in Jean-Christophe Napias and Patrick Mauriès,
The World According to Yves Saint Laurent, 2023.

All I need for my imagination to blend into a place or a landscape is a picture book… I don't feel any need to go there. I have already dreamed about it so much.

As quoted in an interview with *Elle*, December 25, 1995.

This character is extremely contemporary. Madame Bovary expressed women's disarray, which is the same today as it was a century ago.

Yves Saint Laurent discusses his literary inspirations in an interview with Catherine Deneuve, *Globe*, May 1, 1986.

Throughout the latter years of his career, YSL would continue to show two collections a year, drawing on inspiration from the traditional dress of India, China and Russia, as well as artists such as Vincent Van Gogh and literary figures such as Marcel Proust and William Shakespeare.

I am very much alone. I use my imagination to conjure up countries I don't know. I hate to travel. For example, if I read a book about the Indies with photos or about Egypt, where I've never been, my imagination takes me there. That's where I take the best trips.

Yves Saint Laurent discusses the 1982 "India" collection in an interview with Catherine Deneuve, *Globe*, May 1, 1986.

I sought out Japan early on and was immediately fascinated by this ancient and modern country, and ever since I have been influenced by it on many occasions.

As seen on museeyslparis.com.

I am no longer concerned with sensation and innovation, but with the perfection of my style.

Yves Saint Laurent in 1982 on the perfection of his style in the latter half of his career.

Fashion is like a party. Getting dressed is preparing to play a role. I am not a couturier, I am a craftsman, a maker of happiness.

As quoted in *Yves Saint Laurent, 5 avenue Marceau, 75116 Paris* by David Teboul, 2002.

The street had a new pride, its own chic, and I found the street inspiring as I would often again.

Reflecting on this achievements with the "Mondrian" collection, Saint Laurent acknowledges the influence of the Swinging 60s street style. Taken from an article by Frederique Van Reij, *The Rijks Museum Bulletin*, December 2012.

At the age of 47, Saint Laurent was the first living designer to be honoured with a retrospective of his work at the Metropolitan Museum of Art's Costume Institute in New York.

CHAPTER SIX

LEGACY

THE LEGACY OF YVES SAINT
LAURENT IS INDISPUTABLE.

NOT SINCE COCO CHANEL HAD
THERE BEEN A HAUTE COUTURE
DESIGNER WITH AS MUCH
INFLUENCE OVER THE COMMON
WOMAN'S WARDROBE.

WITH OVER 40 YEARS AS A
COUTURIER, IT IS SAFE TO SAY
THAT THERE WILL ONLY EVER BE
ONE YVES SAINT LAURENT.

Jagger: If you weren't a fashion designer what would you do?

Saint Laurent: Live.

As quoted in an interview with Bianca Jagger, *Interview Magazine*, January 1973.

"

I love his subversive approach to
clothes; his dark romanticism with
a hint of perversity. But it's just a
hint – because through his entire
work, collection or images, you
can feel how much he loved and
respected women.

"

Anthony Vaccarello

YSL creative director on the legacy of Yves Saint Laurent. As
quoted in *Vogue Arabia* by Caterina Minthe, April 15, 2018.

On January 7, 2002, an emotional Yves Saint Laurent announced his retirement.

After a 350-piece fashion show of classic designs, the couture house of Yves Saint Laurent closed its doors.

Do not copy Yves. Create your own vision of Yves Saint Laurent, and then follow it.

Pierre Bergé

YSL co-founder to creative director Anthony Vaccarello, as quoted in *Vogue Arabia* by Caterina Minthe, April 15, 2018.

I tell myself that I created the wardrobe of the contemporary woman, that I participated in the transformation of my times.

From Yves Saint Laurent's retirement speech from couture, January 7, 2002.

Saint Laurent is, along with Chanel, the most important fashion designer of the twentieth century.

Pierre Bergé

YSL co-founder, as quoted in an interview with *The Talks*, February 22, 2017.

I have known fear and the terrors of solitude. I have known those fairweather friends we call tranquilizers and drugs. But one day, I was able to come through all of that, dazzled yet sober.

99

From Yves Saint Laurent's retirement speech from couture, January 7, 2002.

> "
>
> I've seen wonderful dresses by Balenciaga and Christian Dior – but the difference between those fashion designers and Chanel and Saint Laurent is that they stayed on the aesthetic field. Saint Laurent and Chanel went to the social field – they changed the lives of women around the world.
>
> "

Pierre Bergé

YSL co-founder, as quoted in an interview with *The Talks*, February 22, 2017.

For a long time now, I have believed that fashion was not only supposed to make women beautiful, but to reassure them, to give them confidence, to allow them to come to terms with themselves.

From Yves Saint Laurent's retirement speech from couture, January 7, 2002.

He pushed his talent to the limit.
He worked so hard, even though
it looked so simple: [his work] was
flawless, he never failed to enhance
the beauty of women.

Vivienne Westwood

As quoted in anothermag.com by Jack Moss, June 1, 2018.

It is cruel: creating things that will never be seen again, things that by their very nature will disappear. Fashion means making things that go out of fashion…

As cited in Jean-Christophe Napias and Patrick Mauriès, *The World According to Yves Saint Laurent*, 2023.

> **"**
> He's got the form of Chanel with
> the opulence of Dior and the wit of
> Schiaparelli.
> **"**

Christian Lacroix

As quoted in anothermag.com by Jack Moss, June 1, 2018.

Yves Saint Laurent died on June 1, 2008, surrounded by partner Pierre Bergé and lifelong friends.

The funeral of the man who changed fashion was attended by over 1,000 people, with the president of France among those to pay their respects.

> ❝
>
> Saint Laurent gave power to women. When a woman was insecure, Saint Laurent garments gave them security. It's true. ❞

Pierre Bergé

YSL co-founder, as quoted in anothermag.com by Olivia Singer, September 14, 2017.

I am the only one left, after forty-two years. The only one still here, still working away. The last couturier. The last fashion house.

As cited in Jean-Christophe Napias and Patrick Mauriès, *The World According to Yves Saint Laurent*, 2023.

I was his first Black muse – he helped open the door for Black models. Sometimes I was his confidante, and I would sometimes inspire his creativity.

Mounia

Mounia was the first Black model for YSL, as quoted in wmagazine.com by Jessica Iredale, August 1, 2008.

"

My first *Vogue* cover ever was because of this man. Because when I said to him, 'Yves, they won't give me a French *Vogue* cover, they won't put a Black girl on the cover,' and he was like, 'I'll take care of that,' and he did.

"

Naomi Campbell

The supermodel thanks Yves Saint Laurent for her first *Vogue* cover, as seen on vogue.co.uk by Leisa Barnett, June 3, 2008.

I think creative people react to
suffering the way they fight death,
making illusions of immortality
we call art.

As quoted in Diana Vreeland et al., *Yves Saint Laurent*, 1983.

Bergé continued to cement the legacy of Yves Saint Laurent, running a foundation that preserved thousands of haute couture garments, accessories and sketches.

"

I'd rather look to the beauty
of the past than the uncertainty
of the future.

"

As quoted in an article by David Livingstone,
FASHION Magazine, 1982.

> ❝
> Chanel and you were the great couturiers of the twentieth century. She of the first half, you the second. ❞

Pierre Bergé

Among Bergé's final words to Yves Saint Laurent at his funeral, June 5, 2008.

In October 2017,
two YSL museums opened
in Paris and Marrakesh,
celebrating the life and
work of Yves Saint Laurent,
one of the most
influential designers of the
twentieth century.

Unfortunately, the true couture client is a dying breed... This is something that saddens me, because my clients were once a great source of inspiration.

"

Saint Laurent on the changing nature of his clientele during the latter years of his career, as seen on theguardian.com by Paul Kelso, January 8, 2014.

"

He was like Picasso… The way he
kept transforming his style, yet each
new one had an incredible impact
on fashion.

"

Valerie Steele

Director and chief curator of the Museum at the
Fashion Institute of Technology on Saint Laurent's artistry, as seen
on showstudio.com by Annabelle Jordan, October 30, 2019.

I, because of luck and instinct,
am one of the last to hold the
secrets of haute couture.

As quoted in Diana Vreeland et al., *Yves Saint Laurent*, 1983.

66

Saint Laurent's body of work is an endless fantasy, a star-filled sky illuminated by a full moon or a midnight sun. Each design reflects its time period, and yet all his creations are modern and timeless.

99

Laurence Benaïm

The biographer reflecting on Saint Laurent's immeasurable legacy, as seen on theglossarymagazine.com by Harriet Cooper, May 7, 2020.

Chanel freed women, and
I empowered them.

As seen on vogue.com by Ellen Burney, January 23, 2019.